The Body Tarot

Celebrate the magic of your body and tap into the wisdom of your subconscious

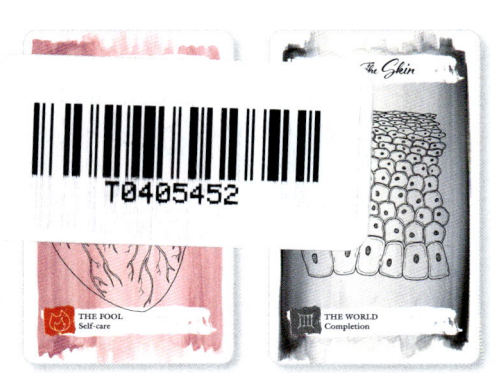

Emma McArthur

CICO BOOKS
LONDON NEW YORK

Acknowledgments

Firstly, thanks to Tania for being my ultimate tarot guru, and for her support throughout this project. Secondly, thanks to CICO Books for turning my idea into a real thing! Thank you to Cindy for taking my idea to the first publishing meeting, Carmel, Sally, and Emily for bringing everything together and making it look amazing, and the RPS and CICO team for taking it into the world. Finally, thank you to Maria, who discovered my drawing materials at the back of the cupboard, and gave me the push I needed to pick up my pens again.

Published in 2022 by CICO Books
An imprint of Ryland Peters & Small Ltd
20–21 Jockey's Fields   341 E 116th St
London WC1R 4BW   New York, NY 10029

www.rylandpeters.com

10 9 8 7 6 5 4 3 2 1

Text and artworks © Emma McArthur 2022
Body artwork on page 14 © Shutterstock.com/eveleen
Design © CICO Books 2022

The author's moral rights have been asserted. All rights reserved. No part of this publication may be reproduced, stored in a retrieval system, or transmitted in any form or by any means, electronic, mechanical, photocopying, or otherwise, without the prior permission of the publisher.

A CIP catalog record for this book is available from the Library of Congress and the British Library.

ISBN: 978-1-80065-096-1

Printed in China

Commissioning editor: Kristine Pidkameny
Senior commissioning editor: Carmel Edmonds
Senior designer: Emily Breen
Art director: Sally Powell
Production manager: Gordana Simakovic
Publishing manager: Penny Craig
Creative director: Leslie Harrington
Publisher: Cindy Richards

Contents

Introduction 4
How to Use the Cards 6
The Three-card Spread 8
The Relationship Spread 10
The Celtic Cross Spread 12
The Five-point Body Spread 14

The Major Arcana 16
0 The Heart 17
I The Bone Marrow 18
II The Arteries 19
III The Veins 20
IV The Brain 21
V The Thyroid Gland 22
VI The Ear 23
VII The Eyes 24
VIII The Teeth 25
IX The Lungs 26
X The Diaphragm 27
XI The Stomach 28
XII The Liver 29
XIII The Pancreas 30
XIV The Spleen 31
XV The Gallbladder 32
XVI The Kidneys 33
XVII The Small Intestine 34
XVIII The Large Intestine 35
XIX The Bladder 36
XX The Muscles 37
XXI The Skin 38

The Minor Arcana 39
The Suit of Wood 40
The Suit of Fire 45
The Suit of Earth 50
The Suit of Metal 55
The Suit of Water 60

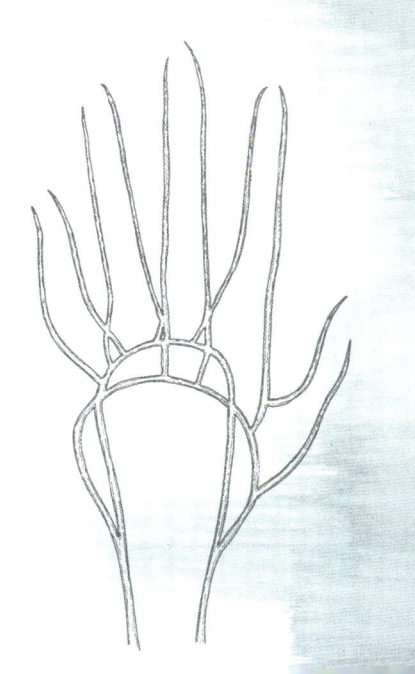

Introduction

Your body is a universe in microcosm. Great galaxies of microbes and shooting stars of neural signals live inside you. You are of miraculous construction and a thing of beauty and wonder.

This tarot deck celebrates the magic of your body and helps you tap into the wisdom of your subconscious through reading these cards. You will learn a bit more about how your body works and how those processes are allegories for the situations we face in our daily lives.

When I first began doing anatomical drawings, I was astounded at the complex structure of our flesh, bones, and blood. The patterns, shapes, and colors enchanted me and I wanted my art to reflect how little we know of our inner workings and introduce that to my audience. It began conversations about the body that showed me that many of us are in the dark about what we actually look like on the inside. This then made me think of how we often do not know the workings of our subconscious mind and we traverse situations reacting instinctively without realizing why we're behaving in a certain way. It seemed to me that the tarot, rather than simply a predictive divinatory system, is also a profoundly useful tool to discover the impulses hidden within us. In this way, the idea of this tarot deck was born.

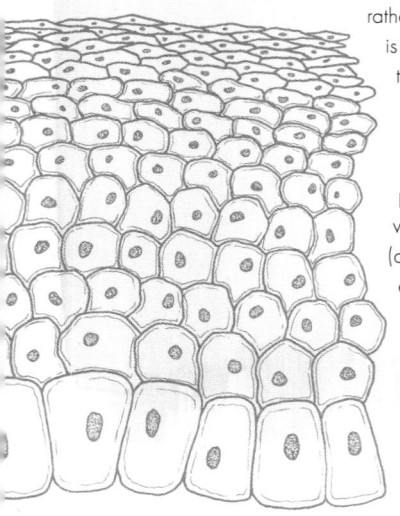

Each organ in the body has a message for us. From our ever-beating hearts to the powerhouse that is the stomach, there is wisdom in not just the spirit of the organ (an idea that Taoist medicine uses to great effect) but also in its biological functioning. For example, the largest organ in our bodies is the skin and it constantly renews itself, sloughing off almost a million dead skin cells every day. When you look at the mirror each morning, you are looking at a completely new face. This can symbolize how we should not fear change and perhaps should think of it more as renewal.

It is my dearest hope that you will find a connection with these cards and can use them to enjoy learning about yourself as well as gain some insights to apply to your daily life.

A deck for everyone

I have not included the reproductive organs in this deck so that it is accessible to all people. The Minor Arcana (see page 39) is based on the elements that appear in Traditional Chinese Medicine, a system that does use the binary female/male (yin/yang) idea, but there is an acknowledgment that both of these energies are in everyone irrespective of how they define themselves.

What this deck isn't

I admire and have been influenced by the beautiful anatomical drawings of Henry Carter that illustrated the 19th century medical reference book, *Gray's Anatomy*. Aspects of this deck also intuitively use some concepts from Traditional Chinese Medicine. However, both Western and Chinese medicine are complex systems that are not based on intuition. If you have medical concerns, please contact your healthcare professional and do not use the deck to attempt to diagnose your problem.

How to Use the Cards

Build a connection to your cards by treating them with respect and handling them regularly. When you're not using them, keep them in a safe place, where they won't be disturbed by the curious. You will find over time that the cards begin to "speak" to you, so you can better understand their response to queries.

The interpretations in this book begin the process of understanding the tarot, but the true secret to knowing the deeper wisdom contained within the cards is to use your own intuition.

ASKING THE RIGHT QUESTIONS

Formulate questions that invite greater insight, such as, "What can I learn from this situation?" or "What do I need to know about this?". Pick the right spread for the question; for example, if you want to know whether someone you're attracted to feels the same way about you, use the relationship spread and ask, "How does [name] feel about me?". Don't ask the cards to predict precisely what will happen, because the future is not fixed. Also, don't ask questions steeped in fear, for example, asking if someone who is ill will die. We will all die one day, so asking questions like this is meaningless and only increases anxiety.

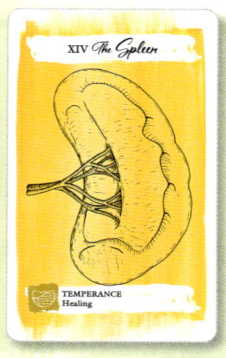

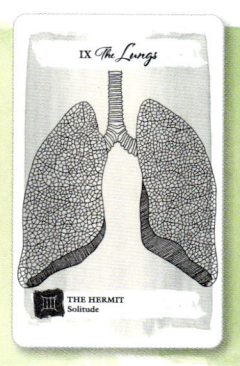

DOING A READING

Shuffle the cards and then cut them twice, each time placing the bottom pile on top, with your non-dominant hand. Fan out the cards, face down, and select the required number for your chosen spread, then lay them out in the spread formation. Only then should you turn them over so you can see the face of each card.

Reading the cards for someone else

Ask the questioner to shuffle the cards and then cut them twice with their non-dominant hand. Fan out the cards in front of the questioner to select the required number for the chosen spread, and ensure they hand them to you one by one, piled one on top of the other. Lay out the cards face down in the spread formation before turning them over.

Always remember to explain that there are no negative cards, only some that indicate challenges to be met, and that nothing is written in stone. As a person's behavior and attitude changes, their cards also change.

The Three-card Spread

This is one of the simplest spreads you can do, showing past influences, your present situation, and the probable future outcome if your attitude or usual way of reacting is followed. Each of these cards will reveal a little more about the query and build into a more complete answer to it.

1
Past influences

2
Present situation

3
Probable future outcome

Card 1: Past influences
This will show you the attitudes, beliefs, and assumptions that influence how you feel about the situation. Read the next two cards in relation to this one. So, for example, if The Large Intestine (see page 35) shows up in this position and The Small Intestine (see page 34) appears in position 3, you are being told to release the fear of the past and show more hope in the future.

Card 2: Present situation
This will tell you if the query is really about one thing or a completely different one. For example, you might have asked about your relationship, but this card seems to relate more to a work situation. After some consideration, you realize that you have been working late recently and it has been affecting your relationship. In that case, it is best to concentrate on whether work is making you happy or if this is the area of life that you should concentrate on improving.

Card 3: Probable future outcome
This shows what will happen if you do not make any significant changes in attitude, behavior, or situation. The card may show a result you would like to happen, so the reading could be telling you to keep doing what you're doing for the outcome you want. However, if this card indicates something you don't desire—for example, a split from your partner—be reassured that you can improve the outcome with a change in yourself and a conscious desire to resolve the problem at hand.

The Relationship Spread

The Relationship Spread can be used to clarify any relationship—not just romantic ones. Perhaps you have a new boss who you don't quite understand yet. This spread will show you what the other person really thinks of you and how you can work to improve the relationship as needed.

1. How you see yourself
2. How you see the other person
3. How you feel about the other person
4. How things are between the two of you
5. Obstacles to the relationship
6. How the other person sees you
7. How the other person feels about you

Note that this spread differentiates between how you see someone and how you feel about them. For example, you may see someone as being arrogant, but you quite like that they seem to have lots of confidence so how you see their personality and how you feel about that are different things. The card in position 4 indicates the current state of the relationship and may highlight any hidden tensions that you may not be aware of. This leads into the card in position 5 and the challenge within the relationship to be overcome. For example, The Ear (see page 23) in this position is quite literally saying you must listen to each other more. The cards in positions 6 and 7 will show you how they see and feel about you—you may be surprised at the divergence between what you think they feel and how they really feel.

1   2

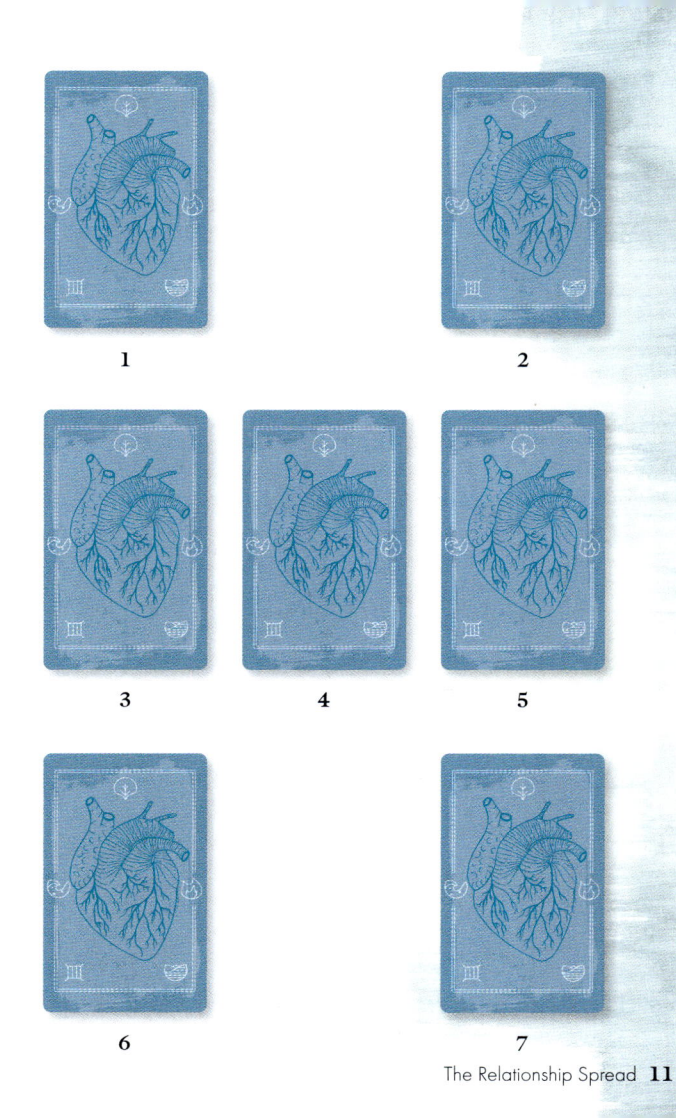

3   4   5

6   7

The Relationship Spread **11**

The Celtic Cross Spread

This is one of the more traditional tarot spreads and is a good one to do once a year when seeking an overview of your life. You can use it for specific questions as well, since it has a great ability to get to the heart of your dilemmas. It is also a good spread to use when reading for others as the card in position 5 will allow you to check if the cards have correctly connected with the querent, since that card will indicate something significant that has already come to pass.

1. The situation right now
2. What is crossing you
3. What draws near
4. The root of the question
5. What has passed
6. What is coming
7. Your attitude
8. External factors
9. Your hopes and fears
10. Outcome if no change made

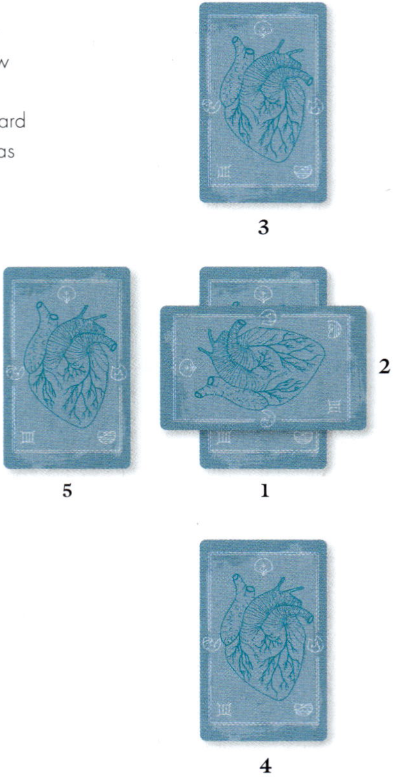

Try and take an overview of the spread when you first turn the cards over. Are there lots of Major Arcana cards? That then means that the querent is going through some big life changes at the minute. Then go on to check what is in each position. The card in position 7 is important as it links to the final outcome card in position 10. If your attitude is inflexible then the outcome will be the one indicated. If you change your attitude, and consequently your actions, the outcome will change too.

If reading for yourself, the hopes and fears position (Card 9) is one that can help you identify your own feelings about a certain outcome. It can be hard when we are in the midst of a situation to discern how we feel about it with any clarity. This is a spread that is useful in that regard.

Finally, you can add depth to your reading by thinking about the elements of each of the cards. For example, lots of Fire cards might be telling you that it is the time to take action.

The Celtic Cross Spread **13**

The Five-point Body Spread

This is an ancient shape that relates to both the five-pointed star and the points of the body represented by the head and four limbs. It is a good spread to use when you want to unlock your subconscious drives. We don't always know why we're conflicted about a situation and this spread helps us to understand what we're not consciously acknowledging.

5

3　　　　　　　　　　2

Questioner

1　　　　　　　　　　4

Center card: Questioner
1. The root of the question
2. Subconscious reactions
3. Conscious actions
4. Helpful influences
5. Final outcome

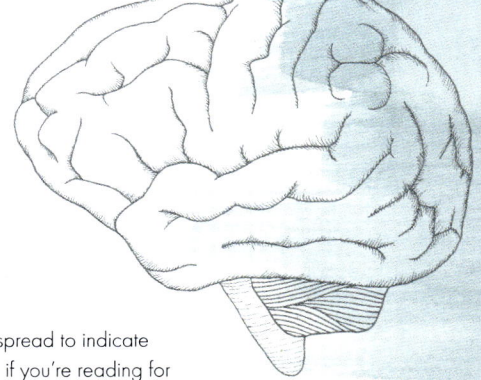

Place a card in the center of the spread to indicate the questioner, which will be you, if you're reading for yourself, or the person asking you to read for them. Having a card in this position—sometimes called the Significator—is useful in order to see how you are perceived by others in relation to this particular query. You can either pick the card that you most feel represents you or you can pick a card at random (which will give you even more of an indication of how you are behaving in this situation).

The Five-Point Body Spread is also the most intuitive of the spreads given here. You may find that rather than the meanings given above, you always find a card in the head position (Card 5) that is at odds with the one in the left-hand position (Card 2), which indicates the heart. In such a case, you are clearly being told to make that famous choice between the heart and the head. Despite what the poets might tell you, the heart isn't always better than the head and, in the end, we always choose what is good for the body as a whole rather than just on the basis of intellect or emotion. Stay focused on what the cards are telling you about both your conscious actions (Card 3) and unthinking behaviors (Card 2), and you will find the right solution.

The Major Arcana

The Major Arcana comprises 22 cards that indicate pronounced life decisions and changes. The cards run from 0 to 21, and each relates to a part of the body as well as the traditional tarot card in that position. If you already read with a more traditional deck, you can draw on your own understanding of those cards too. The element for each card relates to the organ that corresponds to it. The qualities of each element are listed on the table on page 39. This will give you an additional sense of what is at play when you draw that card.

Wood   **Fire**   **Earth**   **Metal**   **Water**

0 The Heart

Traditional tarot card: The Fool

Keywords: Self-care, love, risk-taking, nourishment

Element: Fire

When it comes to pumping blood around the body, the heart pumps blood to itself first and nourishes itself before anything else. This is an important principle when doing anything for others. Self-care or self-love is often confused with selfishness. It is as though we think love or care were finite resources that we run down when concentrating on ourselves, leaving less for others. This is just not true. Instead, think of them as the water in a canal lock going to a higher level. You are the boat that must stay in the chamber while the water rises and lifts you up to the level where you can continue your journey out into the world. The chambers of your heart must also fill up with love for yourself before you can project that love forward onto others.

When this card comes up in a reading, it is often an indication of where you are holding on to vital energy and, perhaps, denying either yourself or others the love and care needed. This is a strong card in relationship readings, but almost always indicates that you need to step back from giving too much of yourself to others. You need to take some risks and begin a journey that will return you to yourself.

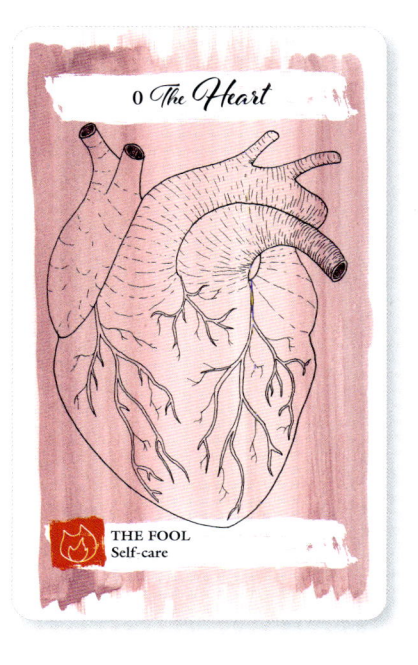

The Major Arcana **17**

I The Bone Marrow

Traditional tarot card: The Magician

Keywords: Alchemy, transformation, benevolent power, potential

Element: Water

Bone marrow is the tissue inside some of your bones, such as the thigh and hip, and it contains stem cells which make more than 220 billion new blood cells every day. Most blood cells in your body come from here. Just as the alchemist unleashes the potential in base metal and turns it to gold, so the bone marrow transforms stem cells that have potential to be anything into your blood. This conjuration in body and spirit is vital to our growth and evolution in life. This card is telling you that you have all the tools at your disposal, but you need to use them effectively.

It also asks you to consider where you are holding back your potential. The body has this power of renewal and creation in its hidden inner workings; in the same way, you may not be able to see what can be created within your consciousness just yet, but it is percolating in the background. Knowing that you have this power to hand should give you the confidence to move forward. If you feel creatively blocked, consider some form of lucid dreamwork to unlock the information you now need. There is help at hand, whether you believe that to be divine intervention or just your own subconscious helpfully furnishing you with an answer.

II The Arteries

Traditional tarot card: The High Priestess

Keywords: Mystery, patience, stillness, enrichment

Element: Fire

The arteries are the blood vessels that carry oxygen-rich blood away from the heart and deliver it to the tissues of the body. We all know the seriousness of damaging an artery. High blood pressure is one way in which this can happen. It requires a calm outlook to avoid that condition, and this is the energy of this card: a patient, peaceful stillness that permits the most enriching, nourishing processes to take place.

When you see this card in a reading, you are being encouraged to take a patient approach while staying alert to opportunities and changes in situation. There are mysterious forces at play here too, so it can seem as though several coincidences collide to give you an almost ordained outcome. The universe is now moving in a way that is for your greater good. You may not be aware of the oxygen that is being delivered to you through the arteries of fortune, but you will certainly see the positive end results.

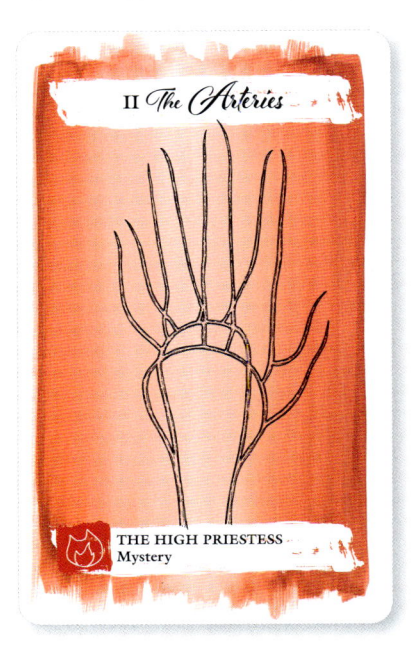

The Major Arcana

III The Veins

Traditional tarot card: The Empress

Keywords: Contentment, satiated, abundance, mothering

Element: Water

After the arteries have delivered precious oxygen to the tissues of the body, the veins take the now deoxygenated blood back to the heart. This incredible flow in and out of the heart is one of the most important systems keeping us alive. We are satiated by the oxygenated blood, content in our health and the abundance we have within our miraculous bodies. In the same way, the appearance of this card denotes a sense of satisfaction with our lot in life. We are enjoying the feeling of nourishment and of being taken care of, in the way a loving mother would take care of a child.

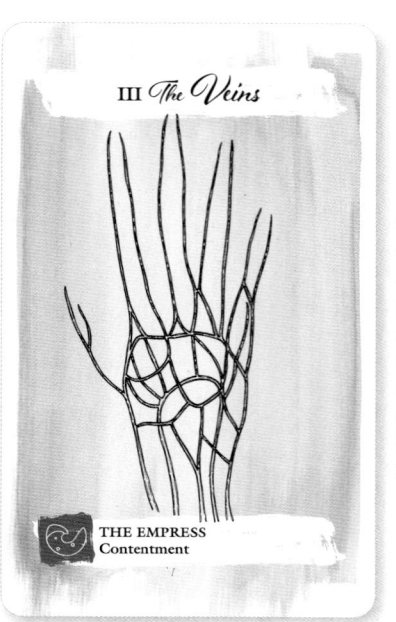

When this card appears in a relationship spread, it almost always denotes a marriage or union of some kind—the end of a dating cycle in a way satisfying to both partners (though, of course, you must also read the surrounding cards to see if this is a positive outcome for all concerned). It is also lucky in answers to questions about money and prosperity as the abundance shown here is of a material, rather than spiritual, nature. The flow of life is soon to bring more oxygen to your finances and restore what has been depleted.

20 The Major Arcana

IV The Brain

Traditional tarot card: The Emperor

Keywords: Authority, nostalgia, action, personality

Element: Fire

The brain in Traditional Chinese Medicine is called the "sea of marrow" and is considered to be linked to, and controlled by, the kidneys. This is why dementia patients are often given kidney-reinforcing herbs when they present to a TCM doctor. However, the brain is not just the preserve of any one organ. It is influenced by the heart and by the stomach. In fact, through neurons (a special type of cell in the brain), all systems of the body communicate with the brain.

In the West, we often consider the brain to be the essence of a person, that the intellect is where the consciousness and, indeed, the soul (if you believe in it) lives. When a person is brain-dead, we pronounce them dead. This means that we give the brain a great deal of authority over us. It is also where memories are processed and so is the seat of nostalgia and our personality.

Seeing this card in a reading reminds us of who we are and encourages us to use our authority over ourselves to ensure that we are doing right by our own talents. It is a call to action in advocacy of our own interests.

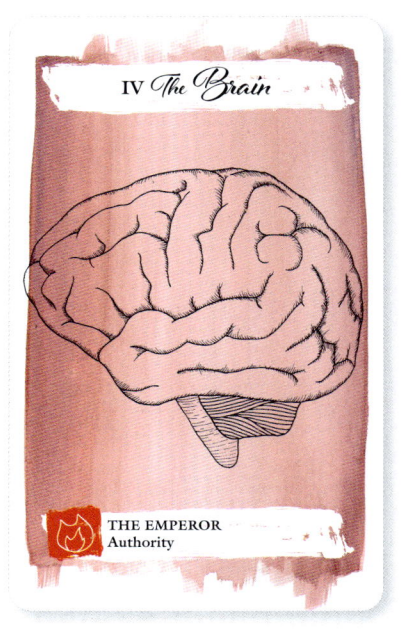

The Major Arcana **21**

V The Thyroid Gland

Traditional tarot card: The Hierophant

Keywords: Community, beliefs, learning, society

Element: Water

The thyroid is a butterfly-shaped gland at the front of the neck. It regulates metabolism and balances hormones. It contributes to an overall sense of well-being. In the way that the thyroid is key in promoting harmony in the body, a single person who selflessly gives of their time is key to a happy community. This card represents the coming together of the querent with others for positive outcomes, whether that is through a spiritual organization, such as a church, youth group, or neighborhood scheme.

There is a strong sense of learning within this card, linking it to younger people. However, it is not just the young who need education: lifelong learning should be the aim of every evolving being. If you're now being approached with an opportunity to learn, the appearance of this card bodes well for the experience being a good one.

This card also might suggest that you have been feeling isolated; the only way out of that is to connect with others, no matter how fearful of rejection you might be. It may be time to spread your wings and push out of your comfort zone.

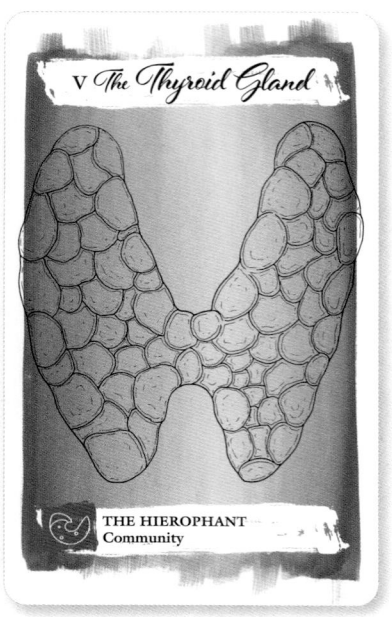

VI The Ear

Traditional tarot card: The Lovers

Keywords: Relationships, desire, values, morality

Element: Water

When we think of the ear, we think of listening, and that is definitely a core requirement in healthy and happy relationships. However, the inner ear is also key in balance. Staying upright literally and metaphorically is indicated by this card. When you consider what your personal values are, you arrive at your own morality and sense of right and wrong. This may not tally with the rest of society's notions about a moral code, but the important thing is that you respect your own decisions in life and stick to your own standard of behavior.

Often a decision or dilemma arrives with this card, and you must consult your rational rather than emotional thoughts on a matter before you decide what to do. When met with two equally desirable outcomes, instead of worrying about what you might be missing, embrace the choice you make as the only path there could have ever been and commit to it passionately and without regrets.

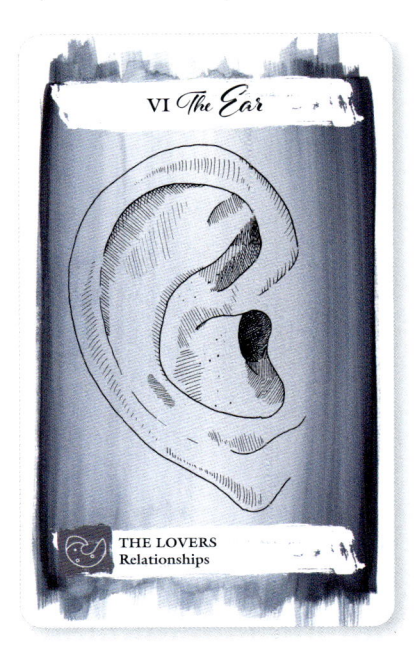

The Major Arcana

VII The Eyes

Traditional tarot card: The Chariot

Keywords: Success, determination, confidence, divine help

Element: Wood

Around 80 percent of our sensory perceptions come from our eyes, if we are sighted. While we often hear the truism that appearances can be deceptive, for the most part, the other saying that "seeing is believing" is the one we follow. This card is telling you that your eyes are not deceiving you and the success you may have been craving is yours for the taking. There is an element of divine help (if you believe in higher powers) or dumb luck (if you don't), but the greater part of the victories indicated by this card will come from grit and faith in your own abilities.

This is the card that comes into play when you can prove to your boss, in solid facts and figures, that you are an asset for the company and deserve that pay rise. It is the card that indicates you have the determination to enable a new venture to succeed. It shows that you're not afraid of hard work and have belief in yourself. It encourages others to see you as you see yourself—in a positive, leadership role. Oddly enough, even if you beat a competitor to a position of power, there won't be fallout from that—your opponent will accept your superior performance.

24 The Major Arcana

VIII The Teeth

Traditional tarot card: Strength

Keywords: Resilience, endurance, tolerance, persuasion

Element: Earth

To get your teeth into a problem means to stick with it, beyond difficulties, to go deeper and aim at a more profound understanding of it. This requires patience and strength of character. If you find this card in a position that indicates you in a spread, you can be reassured that you have all the qualities you need to achieve the outcome you want. This is the card of the calm schoolteacher who can tame the wildest of students through quiet authority. You don't need to "bite" or use manipulation; you have the inner strength to persuade people to see things your way.

The great thing about the energy here is that it isn't the might of the violent military dictator, it is the strength of the parent who still gets up at night to gently put their child back to bed after a long shift at work. It is compassion and love that fights through fatigue and a marathon of activity to meet the end goal. Those blessed by the appearance of this card will be able to access a reservoir of this power.

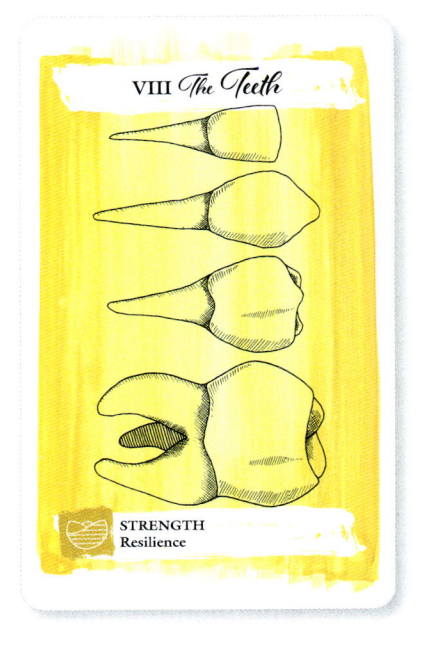

IX The Lungs

Traditional tarot card: The Hermit

Keywords: Solitude, quiet, pilgrimage, wisdom

Element: Metal

Can you feel your lungs? You probably took a deep breath as you read that, but in truth you cannot really feel your lungs because they are a hidden organ in your torso. However, you would immediately know if your lung capacity was compromised. Breathing is something we do without thinking about it, but if we stop breathing, we die. In the same way, we rarely think about those small spaces of time when we are alone because we are not consciously aware that we are alone. In some cases, we avoid that solitude by filling it with smartphones or the drone of a TV or radio. We fear the quiet, as though we shall learn a terrible secret about ourselves in that solitude.

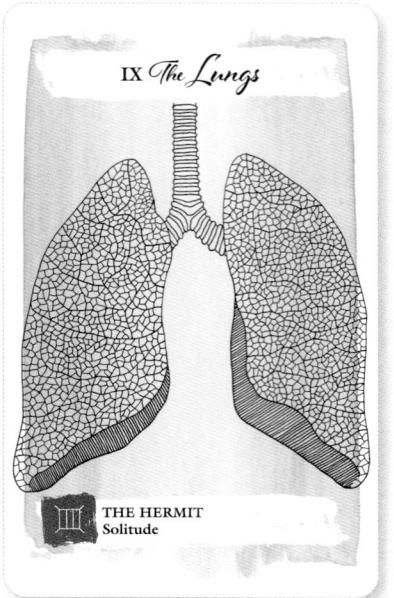

The appearance of this card reminds us that true wisdom lies in seeking the truth, even when it makes us uncomfortable or forces us to have undesirable experiences, such as loneliness or sadness. It is a life skill to learn to sit with unhappiness until it goes away. So many of us believe we are unable to do so, but those who do report back that things are never as final or awful as we think they are. We have the capacity to heal and be happy again, if only we give ourselves the space, silence, and solitude to do so.

X The Diaphragm

Traditional tarot card: The Wheel of Fortune

Keywords: Change, movement, luck, fate

Element: Metal

The diaphragm is a muscle that facilitates your breathing. It is what allows us to breathe in and out. It supports the cycle of the breath, and as such this card supports the cycle of life. If there is one constant in life, it is change. We know that we aren't able to stay children forever—and nor should we want to, given that adulthood brings its own joys. We may (or may not) choose to date and marry and have children of our own, but what is not a choice is the fact that we age and so life stages will come up to meet us, even if we have not prepared for them.

How far you embrace the energy of this card will depend on your feelings about change, because this is the card that turns things upside down. The out-breath must naturally follow the in-breath. Stagnation is bad for everyone, so even if the changes that are coming are not to your liking, you may well look back on this time as a defining period in your life. Alternatively, if you are going through a bad time, this is a wonderful indication that things are about to change. The wheel of fortune is ever turning and good times will be here again. This too shall pass.

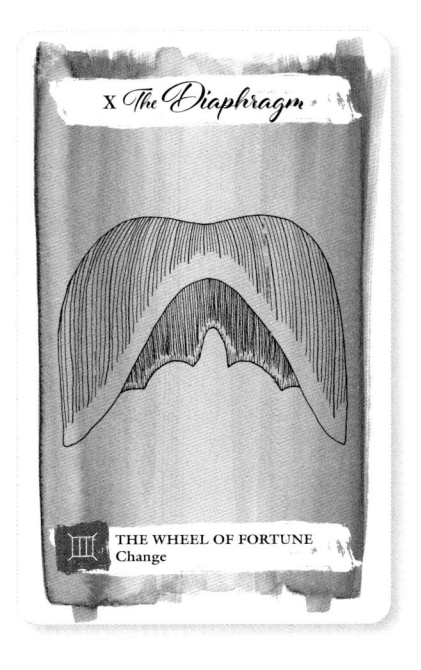

The Major Arcana

XI The Stomach

Traditional tarot card: Justice

Keywords: Fairness, judgment, consequences, legality

Element: Earth

The stomach is the powerhouse of the body. It is now thought that we have a secondary "brain" of sorts in our gut that is responsible for all the processes that happen there. Have you ever eaten something and immediately known you were going to be sick? That's the stomach telling you swiftly what is good for you, because you may have sniffed what you ate and thought it was fine, but the stomach has better judgment than you and has rejected what you ingested. In the same way, this card is about sound judgment and swift decisive action. Society decides together in democratic nations what their laws should be. We then follow those (or not) depending on our personal morality. This card indicates the consequences of our actions, whether that is a broken contract or a criminal act.

This can be a very positive card to draw if you have been the victim of crime, as it can indicate that justice will result, but this interpretation does depend on where in the spread the card lands. In any case, at least you do know that all the arguments will be weighed, and the judgment will be a considered one.

XII The Liver

Traditional tarot card: The Hanged Man

Keywords: Sacrifice, release, contradictions, reflection

Element: Wood

One job out of the hundreds that our livers do is to detoxify and remove that which would harm us. Indeed, the liver performs many functions of which the general populace is unaware. It can regenerate itself if damaged and, in fact, does so every time you drink alcohol because some liver cells die and are replaced, so this sacrifice of itself is a key part of its functioning. Much like this, the liver card encourages useful sacrifice of your own needs for the greater good.

You should also take this card as an invitation to look at things from a different angle and perhaps release something you shouldn't be holding on to in the first place. It is possible to hold a coin in your open palm just as much as it is in a closed fist. There should be no fear of releasing a situation, person, or thing, because if it is destined to be with you, it will always return to you.

This card also tells you to see things from a new perspective at this time and find unusual solutions to problems. Inspiration will strike when you turn things on their head and reflect on the question from a completely novel position.

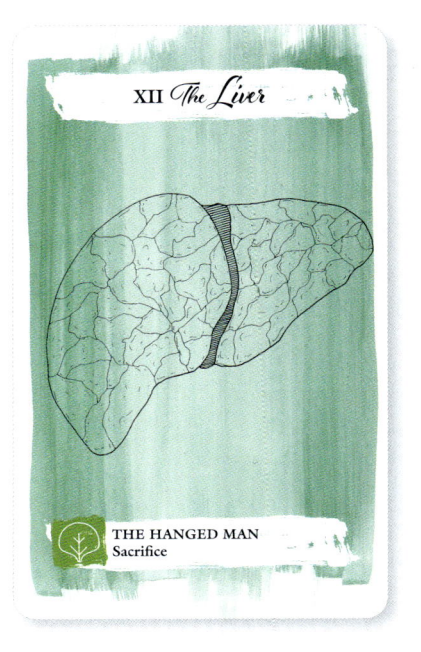

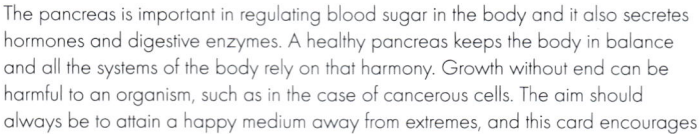

XIII The Pancreas

Traditional tarot card: Death

Keywords: Transformation, endings, decluttering, pause

Element: Wood

The pancreas is important in regulating blood sugar in the body and it also secretes hormones and digestive enzymes. A healthy pancreas keeps the body in balance and all the systems of the body rely on that harmony. Growth without end can be harmful to an organism, such as in the case of cancerous cells. The aim should always be to attain a happy medium away from extremes, and this card encourages us to let go of what is no longer helpful. This may require stillness and a pause in your activity to consider what is really happening in your life—perhaps a retreat would give you the chance to consider your options and end what is harming you and your peace of mind.

While people fear the Death card as meaning the ultimate ending, that is not what is implied here. It is merely a transition or transformation to another stage of life. A divorce can feel like a tragedy or a freeing release. A house move can feel like a sad ending or a bright new beginning. A child leaving home can feel empty or liberating. In truth, these transitions can be a bit of both, but as long as you are kind to yourself and others, you will find it a cathartic experience.

XIV The Spleen

Traditional tarot card: Temperance

Keywords: Healing, balance, moderation, vigor

Element: Earth

The spleen, in the early 17th century, was considered the seat of ill humor and melancholy, so to "vent your spleen" was an expression meaning you aired your anger or negative feelings. However, this is not the truth of this organ. It is vital in fighting infections in the body and promoting tissue healing. Being so key to bringing the body back into balance, this card indicates that a moderate approach is one that is needed now. It is definitely the opposite of venting!

Taking a calm and steady approach will gain the best results and enable you to heal any divisions you are currently experiencing. Cooperation is the name of the game, in the way that the spleen in some systems of healing is said to help the stomach. Join forces with others to create the outcomes you want. Be the person who delivers cohesion through gentle persuasion and loving intent. If you feel there is a sticking point in achieving this, remember that yielding is also an option—and sometimes may be the best one in the long run.

This is also the card that means quite literally temperance, in the sense that it may be time to give alcohol a break for now.

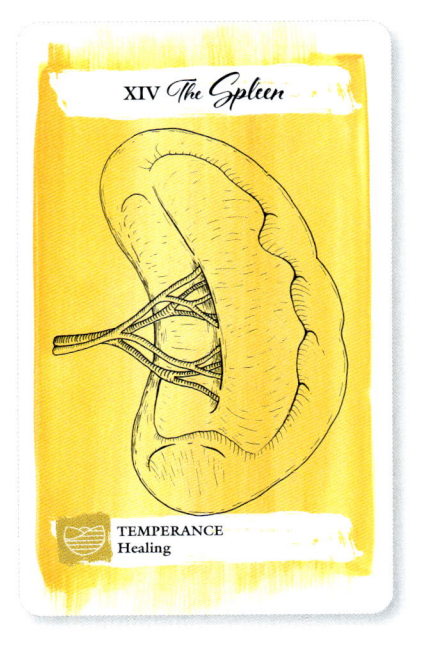

The Major Arcana

XV The Gallbladder

Traditional tarot card: The Devil

Keywords: Enslavement, despair, ignorance, anger

Element: Wood

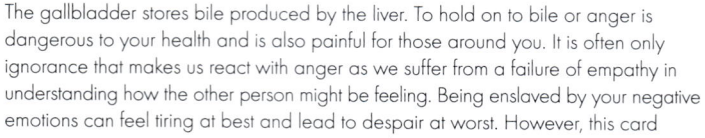

The gallbladder stores bile produced by the liver. To hold on to bile or anger is dangerous to your health and is also painful for those around you. It is often only ignorance that makes us react with anger as we suffer from a failure of empathy in understanding how the other person might be feeling. Being enslaved by your negative emotions can feel tiring at best and lead to despair at worst. However, this card indicates a way around this, and you can release yourself from this situation.

Shining the light of wisdom on a problem will always make anything negative scuttle away. Seeking out therapy or removing yourself from a bad situation is the precursor to solving your problems and having a better experience of life. Simply staying put and stuck in an obsessive trap is not an option—at least, not if you want to restore yourself to happiness. You are not able to control the behavior or choices of others, but you can control how you react and what you do. Make sure that this is to your highest good and work hard to release any residual feelings of anger, betrayal, or hate.

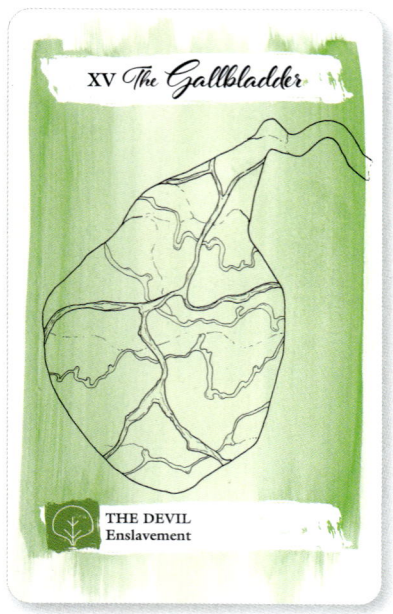

XVI The Kidneys

Traditional tarot card: The Tower

Keywords: Upheaval, crisis, release, cleansing

Element: Water

Your kidneys do the important job of removing waste and excess fluid from your blood. They get filtered out, along with acid, so that your body maintains a healthy balance of water, salt, and minerals. Anyone who has experienced kidney stones knows how painful it can be when waste forms crystals in this organ. In the same way, waste can solidify in your life if you do not cleanse it out. Holding on to grudges, anger, and fear can cause you distress. This doesn't mean one should avoid feeling anything uncomfortable (for example, it is necessary to feel and own your grief), but you shouldn't hold on to those emotions beyond what is healthy for you.

The appearance of this card can indicate a sudden upheaval that will force you to meet a crisis more completely and acknowledge these emotions. Respond to the challenge of this card in a positive, enlightened way and you will come out the other side stronger, healthier, and happier. Stagnate in the pain of the process and it will still have to pass, but with more difficulty and discomfort than necessary.

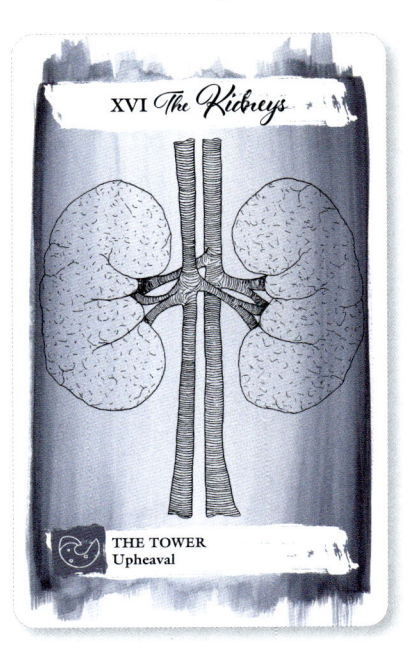

The Major Arcana

XVII The Small Intestine

Traditional tarot card: The Star

Keywords: Hope, calm, clarity, giving

Element: Fire

The small intestine connects the stomach to the large intestine, and it absorbs nutrients and water from the food we eat so that it can be used by the body. This shifting of all that is good and distributing it is the energy of this card. There is abundance at last, after a period of fear and famine. Finally, the storm breaks and a most beautiful dawn appears on the horizon. You can practically smell the hope and potential in the air. Life is great, people are good, and there is nourishment to be had. You can see the path you need to take to meet your goals. This is the inspiration you were seeking, and it has not disappointed everyone.

This is a great card for entrepreneurs beginning on a venture as it indicates a positive boost. There may be practical steps to take and hard work ahead, but for now, look at those rolling green hills and enjoy the lush pastures. As the day turns to dusk, you will know that the star you can see in the night sky is a lodestar for your dreams and a true guide to better times ahead.

XVIII The Large Intestine

Traditional tarot card: The Moon

Keywords: Fear, anxiety, illusions, loss

Element: Metal

The large intestine, sometimes called the large bowel, is the part of the gastrointestinal tract that is responsible for water and salts from material not digested by the body. It is here that feces are formed and eliminated by passing through this organ. This part of you has its own wisdom and is intimately connected with all the other systems of your body, including your brain. Constipation can occur when you are stressed and anxious. Fear causes physical withholding, so this can be a problem at moments when you are worried about failure, such as tests, job interviews, and performances.

However, this card reminds you that your fear is illusionary in that it has no basis in reality. You know you've studied hard enough. You know you're the right candidate for the job. You know you're a star. But it can be hard to get your physical body to acknowledge the facts. Being unable to overcome this feeling can lead to loss in some way, but it should never lead to despair. Thinking things are always going to be hard or stressful is a lie you might tell yourself, but you must use your imagination to remember when things were easier and be comforted knowing that those good times will be here again.

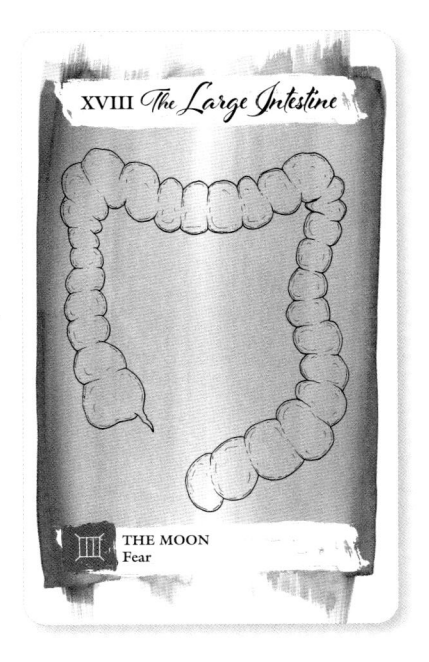

XIX The Bladder

Traditional tarot card: The Sun

Keywords: Energy, radiance, brilliance, enlightenment

Element: Water

The bladder stores urine in the body until it is emptied. In the West, we consider urine to be a dirty substance and it elicits the disgust response in us. In some other cultures, for millennia, urine has been drunk as a form of physical therapy. However, modern Western medicine strongly discourages such practices due to the introduction of toxins back into the body and the strain that puts on our kidneys.

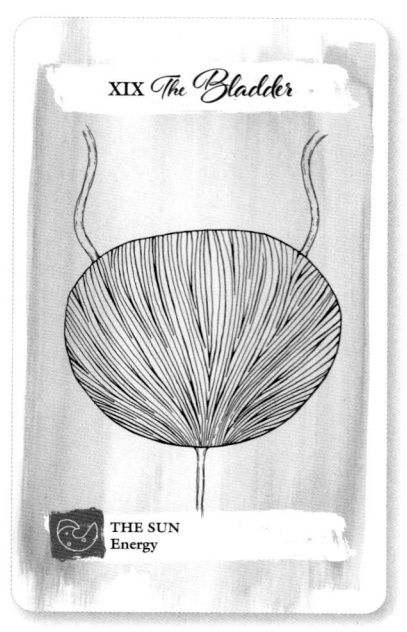

Whichever side we believe, this card is an indicator that health is a priority for you now. It is a great card to draw when coming out of a period of illness, as this means you will release sickness and be restored to health. You now have the energy to do all the extras that we are often encouraged to do, such as exercise and moving your body more. You may find that things that a sun worshipper might enjoy, such as swimming in open water on a sunny day or taking a walk up a sunlit hill, will yield far better results for your health than sweating away in a dark gym. Listen to your body as it has its own wisdom and will guide you back to wellness.

XX The Muscles

Traditional tarot card: Judgment

Keywords: Renewal, calling, reckoning, rebirth

Element: Earth

Muscles are not just the biceps we think of on a gym enthusiast. They help us breathe and defecate, hold us up, support, and moderate—and do the heavy lifting. Muscles are form and function all in one. When we find our purpose in life, we often name that a "calling" and the muscles have answered their calling throughout our bodies. Similarly, this card may indicate that you are being drawn to a career that you previously had no notion of doing.

Receiving this card in a reading allows us to discern for ourselves what is the best way forward. We can exercise our judgment safe in the knowledge that we have the wisdom to make the right choice. That decision will often lead us to a place of renewal and rebirth. It is not always comfortable. If you have been kicking a difficult decision down the path, hoping it will go away, this card says now is the time to deal with it before you store up any more problems for yourself. When you finally commit one way or another, the stars will align to help you see what you knew all along—that you always had the strength within you.

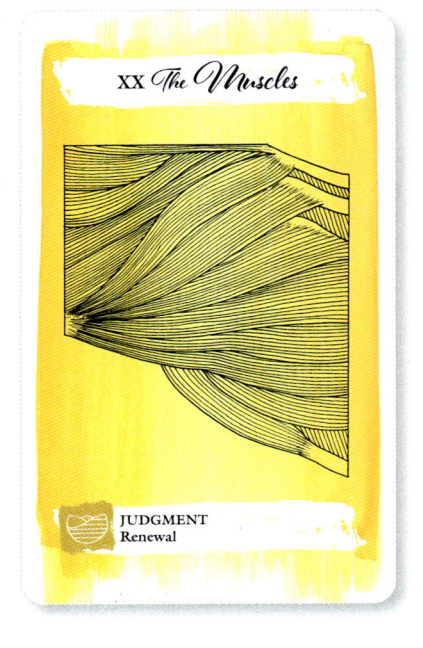

The Major Arcana

XXI The Skin

Traditional tarot card: The World

Keywords: Completion, joy, satisfaction, affluence

Element: Metal

The skin is the largest organ in your body. It encases you and protects you. It keeps you whole. That sense of wholeness or completion is the energy of this card. The world is your oyster, and all is within your grasp. You can enjoy a satisfied sigh and have a period of joyful rest and contemplation about the journey you have been on in life. There is no situation where this card isn't a great sign. Relationships will turn out well. That promotion will be yours. You will complete the triathlon just fine. That doctorate? Not a problem!

However, it can be somewhat overwhelming to get this card and its accompanying blessings. This is where contemplation will help. If your journey has been a hard, poor struggle, you can appreciate the rest and affluence that is now your reality. And perhaps you will enjoy it all the more for what it took to get here.

Appreciation is best shown by helping others and passing on your good fortune, so if you can, once you've enjoyed all the delights of this abundant time, give some of your time to mentoring those who are not quite there yet.

38 The Major Arcana

The Minor Arcana

The 50 cards of this deck's Minor Arcana relate to some traditional interpretations of the four suits of the tarot as well as to concepts from the Five Elements theory (see below). The cards relate to more day-to-day concerns rather than big life changes. Remember to use your intuition to discover what the meanings the cards have for you personally as you develop your reading practice.

Element	Main organ	Secondary organ	Color	Traditional tarot suit	Associations
Wood	Liver	Gallbladder	Green	Swords	Intellectual pursuits, career, thoughts, mental processes
Fire	Heart	Small intestine	Red	Wands	Travel, influences from abroad, creativity, courage
Earth	Spleen	Stomach	Yellow	Pentacles	Money and property, financial health, abundance, prosperity
Metal	Lung	Large intestine	Silver/white	Pentacles	Money from career, ambition, status, inheritance
Water	Kidney	Bladder	Blue/black	Cups	Love and relationships, emotional health, sex, desire

Ace of Wood

Keywords: Birth, beginnings, start

All aces denote a beginning or birth of something. Wood is the element most closely related to spring and new beginnings, so this card may indicate an actual birth, either for you or in your close family and friends. It is a good card for those seeking new employment or embarking on a new venture as it indicates that a start will be made in this area. Fresh beginnings in terms of a new home can also be indicated by this card.

Two of Wood

Keywords: Connection, love, compassion

This card indicates a relationship that is solid and grows over time. It may lack the passion of a first love or the obsession of an unhealthy lust, but it is the sort of love that stands the test of time and leaves both partners enriched and happy. It is the card of long marriage and mutual understanding. If you find you draw this card while suffering problems in a romantic relationship, it urges you to talk things through as you have more in common than you think.

Three of Wood

Keywords: Sadness, heartache, loneliness

There is a saying that into every life some rain must fall, and no card indicates this more than the Three of Wood. There is sadness here, but the state of sadness implies that there is also such a thing as non-sadness or even, dare I say it, happiness. So, while this may be a difficult time, you have the seeds of your own recovery in the dried-out husk that you are presented with. Take heart and know that things will get better.

Four of Wood

Keywords: Rest, patience, strategy

This is not the time to act. Gather your resources and take a moment to ponder your next move. You need time to regroup after a bit of a hard slog at work and emotionally. It may be the ideal time to book yourself a vacation—and if it is one in which you are given large amounts of time to just be and do nothing, all the better. As you regain your energy, so your next adventure will arrive.

The Suit of Wood

Five of Wood

Keywords: Pettiness, struggle, conflict

Avoid office politics and getting drawn into the petty struggles of others. You have a bigger picture in mind and if others cannot see what you are aiming for, then your best bet is to do your own thing as far as you are able to. Removing yourself from those who are petty will always serve you best in the long run. In extreme circumstances, it may even be time to look for another job in order to find a better fit for your values.

Six of Wood

Keywords: Freshness, change, seeking

A change of scenery will do you the world of good, even if it is just a mini break. You have started to feel a little isolated and perhaps even disconnected from your fellow human beings, so going to a place where you need to interact with new people and see new things will refresh your sense of the world and your place in it. If your partner or family are not willing to come along with you, take a leap of faith and go by yourself. You may find you speak to even more people if you are by yourself.

Seven of Wood

Keywords: Liberation, solitude, freedom

Sometimes you need to do things in your own way. Not everyone will understand, and some may even accuse you of not being a team player. Yet you know why you dance to the beat of your own drum—the music is better! Don't feel like you have to conform to anyone else's expectations. In fact, sometimes being on your own schedule can liberate you enough to have really great, life-changing ideas. You may have to return to the fold to convince others to buy in to your idea, but inspiration strikes when you're on your own.

Eight of Wood

Keywords: Trapped, confusion, hampered

There is nothing quite so distressing as feeling trapped and that's the energy this card suggests you are currently experiencing. If you are confused about which way to turn for a solution, you should know that it is not external to you. You are the answer you are seeking. It may sound like hogwash when you're in the midst of a crisis to be told you can pull yourself out of it, but remember that you are far more powerful than you can ever imagine. Look for the solutions in your own emotional armory.

The Suit of Wood **43**

Nine of Wood

Keywords: Worry, sleeplessness, fretting

Spending time fretting never got anything resolved. The American theologian Reinhold Niebuhr wrote the Serenity Prayer, asking God to grant him the serenity to accept that which he couldn't change, courage to change what he could, and wisdom to know the difference. This prayer, even if you're an atheist, is a handy one to remember if this card comes up. We must not expend our energies in worrying about things that can't be changed. Lay down the burden and set yourself free.

Ten of Wood

Keywords: Health, nourishment, support

Tens are cards of completion and so are a handy way of checking if a particular outcome is likely to come to pass (always, always bearing in mind that we have free will and so nothing is ever a foregone conclusion). Wood in the practice of Feng Shui is the element that relates to health and self-knowledge. So, a ten in this suit can mean that you can access great healing in both body and mind, allowing the spirit to feel nourished and supported.

Ace of Fire

Keywords: Inspiration, solution, progress

We've all heard stories of great inventors who only came to the breakthrough in their ideas through a mysterious inspiration in a dream or a fragment of conversation. This is the subconscious diligently working behind the scenes and setting up the answers. In much the same way, this Ace is a source of inspiration, a flash from who-knows-where that enables you to solve that tricky work problem or find the perfect solution to a home dilemma. Welcome this inspiration and you'll find there is more where that came from.

Two of Fire

Keywords: Dominance, partnership, respect

In this deck the Twos represent partnerships, not necessarily romantic relationships but the dynamic when two people interact with each other. A Fire partnership is often characterized by one partner being the bolder or more dominant of the two. You have to be careful not to let a quieter party feel oppressed or subdued by the one who is louder, and perhaps more confident. When that lesson of mutual respect is learned, this is a good pairing for getting creative endeavors off the ground and for bringing life-enhancing projects to market.

Three of Fire

Keywords: Adventure, risk, challenge

The world of adventurers is a strange one. Where others look upon a great mountain or a vast ocean and feel a sense of fear and awe, adventurers see a chance to experience something new... and so they climb, row, or run up to the challenge. In the same way, this card is extolling you to be brave and really go for it. It doesn't matter if you succeed or fail—it only matters that you tried and didn't spend your life wishing for what might have been.

Four of Fire

Keywords: Celebration, joy, happiness

In some countries, the summer is a time of bonfires and celebrations. Prayers are said for a bountiful harvest. That sense of a community coming together to celebrate and ask for the good of the land is the energy of this card. It may indicate weddings or even just a family party for no reason at all. Either way, it signals a time of laughter and a light heart, so enjoy it with your loved ones.

Five of Fire

Keywords: Irritation, impatience, misunderstanding

Sometimes irritations come thick and fast. It can seem as if everything is going wrong and you compound the problems by reacting in an impatient way. The way to deal with the unhelpful energy of this card is to slow down, take a breath, and never forget your compassion for others and, equally importantly, for yourself. Make sure that everything you say and do is properly thought through rather than doing anything off the cuff. This is a time of misunderstandings and cross-purposes.

Six of Fire

Keywords: Triumph, victory, awards

Hurrah! You won the award! There is a triumphant feel to this card, as though someone has garlanded you in victory and you're being carried aloft on shoulders through the town. We are often taught to brush away our successes in order to remain modest and humble, but if we do not acknowledge our wins, why should we strive so hard for them? This is not the time to hide your light under a bushel; accept your accolades graciously and with pleasure. They are well deserved.

The Suit of Fire 47

Seven of Fire

Keywords: Fight, oppression, injustice

Sometimes you have a fight on your hands: a new boss making life difficult for you; a scary new political party about to wrestle power forcefully; perhaps a bully at work. Our lives are varied and can be full of dramatic fights, both small and large-scale. This card shows that you are willing to take a stand and show the courage of your convictions. While conflict isn't pleasant, it is sometimes necessary if we are to fight against injustice or cruelty. If you are sure that you are on the right side of a fight, this card is telling you to stand your ground.

Eight of Fire

Keywords: Action, doing, creating

So, you have a half-written novel at the bottom of a drawer or you have a great idea for an engineering solution, but you're just not making the time to get it developed. This is the card of swift action and it says that the universe helps those who help themselves. Never making it out the starting block and complaining about those who do is never a good approach. Take this as a warning that you must fulfil your creative destiny before it is too late and your idea has been manifested by someone else.

Nine of Fire

Keywords: Mistrust, fear, suspicion

If you have been hurt in the past, it can take a long time to learn to trust again. This card can put in an appearance when you are hesitant about the motivations of others and suspect them of foul play. It is important in this instance to look at where you may be attributing cunning and ill intent where there is none. If you find it nigh on impossible to stop assuming the worst, this is a good time to step back and work on that aspect of your psyche. It is true that you can encounter people who want to take advantage of you, but if you assume that as a default position, you will miss out on a lot of great connections.

Ten of Fire

Keywords: Burnout, tired, overwhelming

A card of completion, the Ten of Fire can feel as though you are about to collapse under the weight of all your obligations. From domestic commitments to a busy work life to all those extra projects we take on as passions, our energy levels can suffer from being overstretched. It may be time to sit down and make a list of everything you are doing or want to do and begin stripping it back by delegating, scheduling a time for completion, or simply letting it go as something that will not be achieved in the near future.

The Suit of Fire

Ace of Earth

Keywords: Payoff, investment, success

Forming a twin with the Ace of Metal (see page 55), this Ace indicates a financial opportunity, but while the Metal Ace is an opportunity that arises from luck, this one is from hard work. You have put in the hours, you know your stuff, and it is now paying dividends in the form of new ways to show off your expertise. You should also keep your eyes open for anything practical you can do to contribute to your material success. Will you earn more if you do a particular qualification? This is the time to invest in it, because it is likely to pay off.

Two of Earth

Keywords: Fun, leisure, enjoyment

This is a card for the start of a relationship that is enjoyable and light-hearted—whether romantic or platonic. You can now find much to laugh about together and have wonderful times together. If it is a romantic relationship, you may find that you then need to restore balance in your life by remembering that you have family and friends and not ditching them for this new love interest. It may require a spot of juggling, but it will be worth it for an emotionally satisfying experience of life.

Three of Earth

Keywords: Teamwork, groups, social

While sometimes it is good to go your own way, this card suggests you work in a team or group to meet your goals. This may be social in terms of a church or community group, or it may be domestic by teaming up with your life partner and children to complete a shared project, such as fixing up your garden. It could also be at work, when working with others will get the job done quicker and with more expertise. Whichever sphere of life it is in, teamwork makes the dream work here.

Four of Earth

Keywords: Greed, scarcity, fear

There is an old saying that "what is for you will never pass you," meaning that fate will ensure that the relationship, career, or luck that is your due will find its way to you, no matter what. However, some people do not trust the universe in that way, and they hold on jealously with both hands to what they have, while looking at how they can obtain more. What are you holding on to too tightly? This may be the time to think about loosening your grip and trusting that you will not be abandoned or left destitute if you exercise some generosity of spirit.

The Suit of Earth

Five of Earth

Keywords: Poverty, loss, lack

Poverty can seep into your bones. It is a hard, grinding, ever-present sickness in the pit of your stomach that is recognizable to anyone who has ever been unlucky enough to experience it. Thankfully, this card does not mean you'll suddenly have to go through that terrible time yourself, but it can denote financial setbacks or perhaps even places where you are emotionally impoverished. Focusing with gratitude on what is going right in your life can often be enough to upend this run of bad luck and, at any rate, it is only temporary.

Six of Earth

Keywords: Generosity, humility, charity

To give is to receive. Anyone who has felt the glow of knowing you got exactly the right present for a family member knows this, as does the person who did the sweaty sports challenge to raise money for the local children's hospital. There is a sense of satisfaction you get from knowing that you have contributed. This card indicates that soon you will have enough to meet your needs and can then give to others. Staying humble in all you do will ensure that you give in an admirable rather than conspicuous way.

Seven of Earth

Keywords: Achievement, ambition, striving

Have you ever undertaken a big project? One so big that at times you couldn't see the end of it at all—something like a house renovation, a large acquisition, or a complex work campaign? When you finished, didn't it feel amazing to look back on it and see all that you had achieved in getting it done? Some will pause at this point and enjoy that feeling. Others will be tempted to tinker and continue on as if nothing were finished at all. Don't be the tinkerer.

Eight of Earth

Keywords: Craft, knowledge, skill

A skilled craftsperson bent over their work is a joy to behold. They have muscle memory for how things are done and years of experience to know how far to hit a nail or shave off a piece of wood. This sort of knowledge is hard-won, requiring years of patience and effort. This attention to detail and expertise is what is required of you now. Don't rush through and hope for the best—you need to put in the time in order to reap the rewards that this card promises to deliver.

The Suit of Earth

Nine of Earth

Keywords: Freedom, comfort, beauty

The arts are something precious to us all. If we did not have movies, theatre, art, books, and music, the world would be a dull place to reside in. This card is superb for those worrying that they have to lose their artistic side in the pursuit of a wage that they can live on. It frees you up to pursue creativity because benefactors and patrons are around the corner. This does not mean you can suddenly become extravagant in your spending, merely that your needs will be met—so it may be time to crack out those paints or that violin.

Ten of Earth

Keywords: Wealth, opulence, tradition

The Ten of Earth is a card of wealth and opulent success. However, it is also about sticking to tradition, so it may well be that whatever is considered the traditional profession for your family is the one where your fortune lies—this applies irrespective of whether your family are in a societally traditional profession, such as law or medicine, or are bohemian artists. Follow in their footsteps, either way, for achievements galore. Once you achieve success, you should also keep one eye on the future and how you can capitalize on your accomplishment.

Ace of Metal

Keywords: Harvest, abundance, luck

Metal is the element that is connected with harvest time and so these are the cards of abundance and luck. The Ace here is for financial opportunities that come your way through good fortune rather than hard work. The feeling is one of being in the right place at the right time. There are those who say you make your own luck, and it is true that a person who goes to industry events is more likely to have "luck" than someone who stays aloof, but it is surprising how often this card brings a spot of luck to just about anyone.

Two of Metal

Keywords: Boldness, cleverness, risk

A bird in the hand is worth two in the bush. That saying could be reversed for this card, as the two in the bush (not yet caught) are the ones you should go for. Sometimes taking a risk is a foolish endeavor, but if you have done your research, the energy of this card supports not playing it safe and striking forward in a bold way. This isn't an excuse to put all your savings on a card game; more that if you take a considered risk, such as an expansion of your business, it is likely to pay off.

The Suit of Metal 55

Three of Metal

Keywords: Windfall, inheritance, compromise

An inheritance or windfall may be on the way for you. How you invest it will have a far-reaching influence, so it is best to consider things carefully. A second home abroad or improvements to your existing property are both good ideas for a sensible use of the funds. However, if arguments arise with others as a result of the choices you make, it is best to reach a compromise rather than sour relationships over money.

Four of Metal

Keywords: Acumen, conscious, choices

Have you ever stuck with lottery numbers because you superstitiously believe that the second you change or stop playing them, the numbers will come up? This is what you're being counselled not to do through this card. Take a close look at your finances and plug any holes that are there just because you've always done it or signed up for it. Make conscious money decisions and you will attract greater luck to yourself.

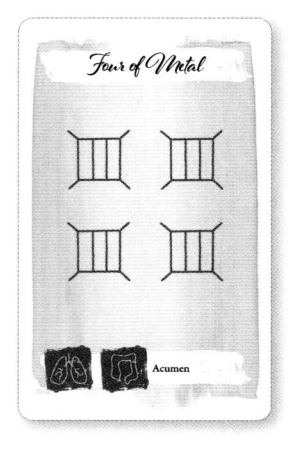

Five of Metal

Keywords: Budget, carefulness, management

Being generous is a definite virtue, but not at the expense of your own future or that of your family. Remember to make a budget and stick to it so that you can still enjoy social occasions, such as throwing a party, without compromising your long-term money goals. You may find that because you are fairly fortunate with money, you take it for granted and that is to be discouraged, no matter how wealthy you are.

Six of Metal

Keywords: Partnership, budgeting, decisions

Relationships can be fraught and one of the things that partners most argue about is money. The best way to avoid that is to have honest discussions about what money means to you and your values with regards to it. Would you feel comfortable having a joint account? Do you prefer to keep all your finances separate? This should not be an exercise in blame or control (a red flag in any relationship), but an honest appraisal of how your money mindsets fit together.

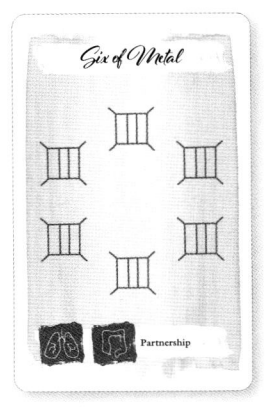

The Suit of Metal

Seven of Metal

Keywords: Resolution, family, solutions

Sibling rivalry can often take on quite epic proportions. If you find that you are frustrated by differences between you, you should consider booking a family holiday. That may have elicited a yelp of protest, but the truth is that we often expect things to be awful without having first given them a chance. If a holiday is a step too far, book a nice lunch on neutral ground such as a restaurant or café and try to mend your relationship that way.

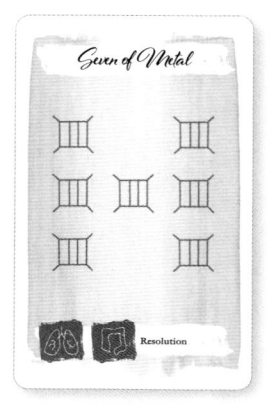

Eight of Metal

Keywords: Home, energy, blessings

This is the card of prosperity at home. Your home should be your haven, so if it is starting to look a little unloved because you are spending so much time out of it, try to schedule some time to feather your nest and make it comfortable and enjoyable to be in again. A well-loved home attracts more abundance and blesses the people who live in it. If you'd like to work with energies in the home, try the Chinese practice of Feng Shui.

Nine of Metal

Keywords: Luck, celebration, prudence

It's time for a party! The Nine of Metal brings the sort of luck that you just have to celebrate. Whether you drink or not, it is the sound of popping champagne corks and expensive dinners. Of course, if you do drink, you'll know that a hangover often accompanies such celebrations the next day, so do keep an eye on how you spend that work bonus or casino win, as you'd hate to get a financial hangover afterwards.

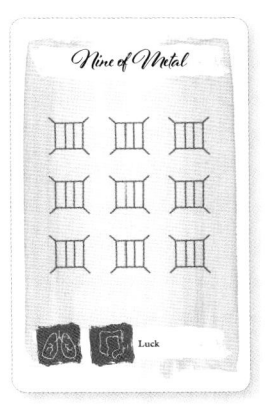

Ten of Metal

Keywords: Charmed, fortunate, blessed

The completion card for this element is one that screams "all good things!" It is luck in its purest sense and is the indication of a charmed life where things seem to fall in your lap. You may not recognize it if your idea of being charmed is all yachts and mansions, but if you've always found yourself in work and have a loving partner and good health, you've won all the cherries in the slot machine. Appreciate your good fortune so that it sticks around, and the yachts and mansions will follow.

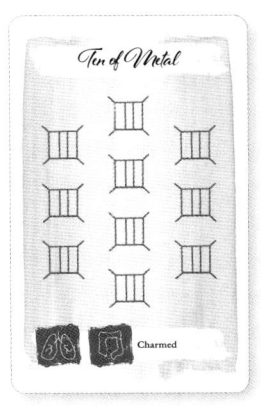

Ace of Water

Keywords: Love, maternal, change

This card reveals the beginning of a new loving relationship—but not necessarily with a new person. It may well be that your existing relationship undergoes a sea change to be even better than it was before. Use your intuition to give you clues as to where you can show more love to yourself and others, and this will enhance the love energy of this card. This card also strongly indicates mothers, so if your relationship with your mother is complicated, this Ace coming up in a spread suggests looking at that in more detail.

Two of Water

Keywords: Ease, happiness, romance

When you think of the great romantic stories of the world, you may be struck by how many of them end in tragedy. It seems as though we think that true romantic love must be cursed in some way. Nothing can be further from the truth. The love this card represents is the one we all crave, and nobody gets poisoned, bitten by an asp, or bricked up into a wall. It is an easy, happy love that you can achieve if you want to—although it can also indicate a happy self-love if you choose not to couple up.

Three of Water

Keywords: Friendship, commonality, fellowship

If the Two of Water (see opposite) is romantic love, then the Three is the card of friendship. We often talk of the friendship zone as if it is a bad place, somewhere to be relegated to if our desired relationship does not come to pass, but friendships are among the most important relationships we form in life. Close friends can become like family, while also providing a place to safely complain about your actual relatives. This card encourages you to appreciate your friendship groups and ensure you are not letting other parts of your life cause you to neglect them.

Four of Water

Keywords: Stagnation, reflection, self-absorption

Ensure you are not getting stuck in a rut by opening yourself to new experiences. Your emotions may be very focused on your inner life at the moment, but that might mean that you are missing the things going on around you. It is fine to have a period of respite from worldly cares, but if you find that you are no longer getting enjoyment in your daily routine, this is a sign that you need to spice things up again with a bout of being social and talking to others. Awaken your curiosity for the world again.

The Suit of Water

Five of Water

Keywords: Grief, loss, process

Grief can be hard to process, and we often want to rush past it. However, it has a terrible habit of returning to us. The smell of our loved one's perfume, a book they raved about, or even a foodstuff you never eat but which has you in floods of tears because the person you have lost once bought it by accident. Try to process any sense of loss that you have been brushing under the carpet. It may not be about death—you could be grieving for a choice you made that closed a door. Whatever it is, once you work through it, you will find contentment on the other side.

Six of Water

Keywords: Innocence, bliss, confidence

If you have seen a child dancing with no self-consciousness, you have witnessed the energy of this card. It is a joyful, innocent, blissful pleasure that we should all be able to access whenever we want. However, as adults we forget this legacy and we become terribly serious. This card gives you permission to release any starchy regard for what people think and "dance like no-one is watching." This may be difficult to do if you've kept yourself buttoned up for a long time, but you may find that situations arise now that give you the same kind of emotional joy.

Seven of Water

Keywords: Rationality, prudence, considering

Have you ever held out for a better offer, only to find you lost the one you had in hand? This card calls for decisions to be made rationally and without dreamy fantasies. Just because someone told you that they heard of a house that sold for twice what yours is worth in your area last month does not mean that you will achieve the same price. Don't let the stars in your eyes blind you to what must be done in the here and now. The more you can keep yourself from daydreaming and stick to the facts, the better the outcome will be.

Eight of Water

Keywords: Movement, change, appreciation

When things end, most people fall into two camps: the ones who hate change—and will be upset for quite some time, trying desperately to hold onto people, places, and emotions that have run their course—and those who move on, appreciating what was but understanding that it is no longer so. To be able to move on from things that have finished is a sign of maturity, but one that we often do not recognize as such. We may think it shows heartlessness; on the contrary, it creates space for more heart-filled experiences.

Nine of Water

Keywords: Manifestation, desire, fulfillment

This is the card that you want to come up when you have just blown out the candles on your birthday cake. It is a card of desires met and wishes fulfilled. The trouble is that sometimes you have to be very careful about what you wish for. This is not superstition. It is merely a warning to keep your eyes open so that you are sure that the gorgeous person you want to date is worthy of you and that the house you want to buy is not a money pit. If you've done your research, then all will be well.

Ten of Water

Keywords: Happiness, joy, ease

I call this card the "happily ever after" card, as it gives an indication of a period of joy and happiness. It is a picture-perfect Christmas or a beautiful summer wedding. However, we all know that the world is in flux and "ever after" is not forever, all families row at Christmas, and there is always a drunk relation falling into the cake at weddings. If you can stay easy-going about the things that can—and do—go wrong at times, the end result may not be perfect, but this card says it will come pretty darn close.